# IMMUNOLOGY

# THE SCIENCE OF THE HUMAN BODY

# BODY SYSTEMS

# CELLS, TISSUES & ORGANS

# DISEASES

# EPIDEMICS & PANDEMICS

# GENES & GENETICS

# IMMUNOLOGY

**MASON CREST**
450 Parkway Drive, Suite D, Broomall, Pennsylvania 19008
(866) MCP-BOOK (toll-free)

James Shoals

First printing
9 8 7 6 5 4 3 2 1

ISBN (hardback) 978-1-4222-4196-7
ISBN (series) 978-1-4222-4191-2
ISBN (ebook) 978-1-4222-7615-0

Cataloging-in-Publication Data on file with the Library of Congress

Developed and Produced by National Highlights Inc.
Interior and cover design: Torque Advertising + Design
Production: Michelle Luke

# THE SCIENCE OF THE HUMAN BODY

# IMMUNOLOGY

JAMES SHOALS

MASON CREST

# KEY ICONS TO LOOK FOR:

 **Words to Understand:** These words with their easy-to-understand definitions will increase the reader's understanding of the text while building vocabulary skills.

 **Sidebars:** This boxed material within the main text allows readers to build knowledge, gain insights, explore possibilities, and broaden their perspectives by weaving together additional information to provide realistic and holistic perspectives.

 **Educational videos:** Readers can view videos by scanning our QR codes, providing them with additional educational content to supplement the text. Examples include news coverage, moments in history, speeches, iconic sports moments, and much more!

 **Text-Dependent Questions:** These questions send the reader back to the text for more careful attention to the evidence presented there.

 **Research Projects:** Readers are pointed toward areas of further inquiry connected to each chapter. Suggestions are provided for projects that encourage deeper research and analysis.

## QR CODES AND LINKS TO THIRD-PARTY CONTENT

# CONTENTS

# GERMS

Our body works very hard in digesting food, pumping blood, giving us energy to do our various daily activities. However, at times our body fails to carry out its functions properly. This may happen due to various reasons. Some of our organs may fail to perform well because of an injury whereas some might be infected by germs.

## What are Germs?

Germs are tiny organisms which enter our body and can cause various diseases. They can be called "invaders," which enter our bodies and cause diseases. Germs are very small in size. Due to their small size, we are unable to see them with our naked eyes. Instead, we need a microscope to see them. That is why germs are sometimes referred to as microscopic. Germs are so small in size that they creep into our bodies without being noticed.

 **WORDS TO UNDERSTAND**

**diphtheria:** a serious bacterial disease that makes it difficult for the person to breathe.

**immune system:** part of the body that works to protect from illness.

**pertussis:** a serious bacterial disease that causes excessive coughing.

**vaccination:** a medical treatment that helps the body resist disease.

## Type of Germs

Germs are present everywhere: in the air, on the surface of our body, inside the body, in soil, on toys, floors, and counters. The four major categories of germs include: bacteria, viruses, fungi, and protozoa. They can enter into plants, animals, and humans, and can cause various diseases. These germs spread through air or by touch.

If someone is suffering from a cold, his sneezing spreads germs in the air. This is how other people also catch the cold by coming in contact with a sick person.

## How do Germs Cause Disease?

Germs multiply once inside our body. They start eating up the nutrients, consuming the energy of the cells, and producing toxins. These toxins are poisonous and cause infections in the body, which may result in sniffles, flu, or vomiting. In response to these infections, our immune system springs into action and activates our white blood cells. For instance, in fighting off the common cold, the body might react with fever, coughing, and sneezing.

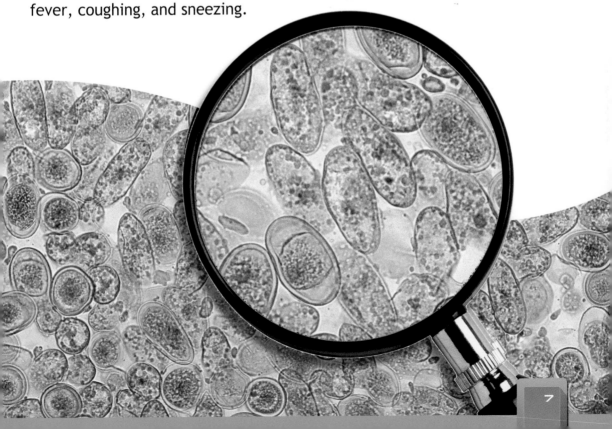

## Protection against Germs

Most germs are spread through the air by sneezing or coughing, and touching. We can protect ourselves from various infections by following certain simple methods. Handwashing is one of the easiest and most effective ways to protect oneself from germs and most infections. Wash your hands before preparing or eating food, eating and drinking, feeding an infant, tending to sick person(s), treating a cut or wound, touching contact lenses, after coughing or sneezing, changing a diaper, and using the toilet.

Vaccination is also considered as the best defense against certain diseases. Many vaccines are given in childhood to provide protection against infections like diphtheria, pertussis, and others. Adults, however, still need to be routinely vaccinated to prevent some illnesses, such as tetanus and influenza. Medicines offer protection against particular germs. For example, an antiparasitic medication might keep you from contracting malaria if you travel to or live in a risk-prone area.

## SIDEBAR: DID YOU KNOW?

- Our body sheds millions of skin cells everyday.
- The "dust bunnies" below your bed are much more than dust. They also contain your hair and sloughed-off skin cells.

# BACTERIA

Bacteria are small one-celled organisms found everywhere in and around our body. They are relatively simple organisms, and are extremely small; a pinhead may have millions of bacteria on it. Under the microscope they may appear as rods (bacilli), sphere (cocci) or spiral (spirilla) shaped. They need food, water, warmth, and time to grow.

## Types of Bacteria

Bacteria are categorized into two types: archaebacteria and eubacteria. Archaebacteria are those bacteria that survive in extreme conditions, such as in Antarctica or under deep sea. Some examples of archaebacteria are methanogens, thermophiles, and halophiles. Eubacteria reside in human skin and cavities. They can cause soft tissue infections.

## WORDS TO UNDERSTAND

**budding:** a form of asexual reproduction in which an organism reproduces by itself.

**chemosynthesis:** the process in which certain organisms make food without the help of sunlight, using carbon dioxide and water.

**DNA:** deoxyribonucleic acid is a substance containing genetic information and is present in all living organisms.

**enzymes:** a chemical that triggers, or increases the rate of, a reaction.

**fragmentation:** a type of asexual reproduction in which part of an organism if cut can grow into a new organism.

**nucleic acid:** a liquid (in the form of DNA/RNA) that is found in the cells of all living beings.

## Nutrition in Bacteria

In order to live, bacteria obtain their nutrition from the environment in which they reside. In some cases, that environment is the human body. Most bacteria are heterotrophic, which means they cannot manufacture their own food. Autotrophic bacteria, on the other hand, can manufacture their own food by the processes of photosynthesis and chemosynthesis.

## Reproduction

Bacteria can reproduce outside or inside the body, and cause infections. The genetic material of bacteria is organized in a circular strand of DNA. Bacteria grow to a fixed size and then reproduce or divide by binary fission in order to yield identical daughter cells. Some bacteria reproduce by budding or fragmentation.

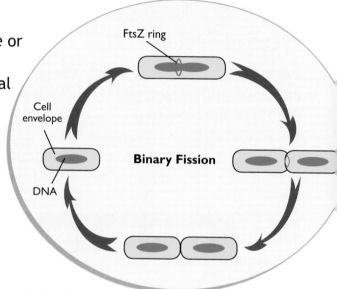

FtsZ ring

Cell envelope

DNA

Binary Fission

Some bacteria are capable of specialized types of genetic recombination, which involve the transfer of nucleic acid by individual contact (conjugation), exposure to nucleic acid remnants of dead bacteria (transformation), exchange of plasmid genes, or by a viral agent (transduction). Under unfavorable conditions, some bacteria develop highly resistant spores with thickened coverings, called endospores.

## Benefits of Bacteria

Some bacteria are good for the body. For instance, bacteria living in our intestines produce several enzymes necessary for the building up and breaking down of organic compounds. They also help us use the nutrients in the food we eat and make waste from what's left over. Other bacteria are used for soil enrichment with crops, for food preservation by pickling, and for decomposition of organic wastes in septic tanks or some sewage disposal plants. Some bacteria are also used by scientists in labs to produce medicines and vaccines.

## Effects of Harmful Bacteria

Some bacteria are harmful as they are a cause of several diseases not only to humans but to plants as well. Typhoid, cholera, tuberculosis, pneumonia, and plague are some of the diseases caused due to bacteria. Many of them are infectious. Harmful bacteria can even spoil our food.

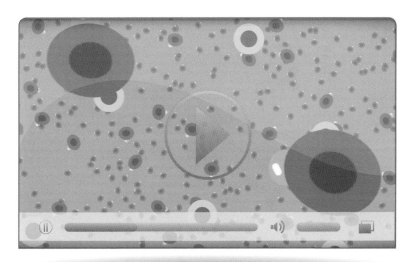

Watch this clip for information about how bacteria can make you sick.

 SIDEBAR: DID YOU KNOW?

- Penicillin was discovered by Alexander Fleming in 1928. The first antibiotic to be discovered, it was the by-product of a fungus called *Penicillium notatum*.
- There are millions of bacteria in one gram of soil.

# VIRUS

Runny nose, red eyes, and sore throat are some symptoms of the common cold. It is caused due to some very microscopic particles known as viruses. A virus is an infectious agent that multiples inside the living cells of an organism. Generally, viruses cause the most common respiratory problems like the flu, the cold, and bronchitis. Some very deadly diseases like hepatitis and AIDS are also caused by certain types of viruses.

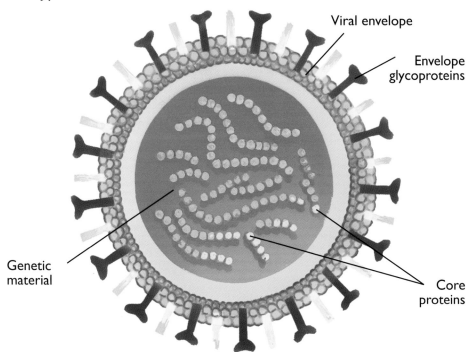

Viral envelope

Envelope glycoproteins

Genetic material

Core proteins

 **WORDS TO UNDERSTAND**

**dormant:** describes something alive but inactive.

**hepatitis:** a medical condition of the liver which causes swelling and inflammation.

**host:** here, the body in which a virus reproduces and causes disease.

# Viral Sickness

Viruses do not require food to eat and do not produce any waste. They even don't respire like other living beings. They represent the smallest forms of life and act as the connecting link between the living and the nonliving. The only living characteristic they show is reproduction in the body of the **host** with the help of the host's DNA machinery. Once inside the host, viruses multiply and produce disease. It may appear that they are not alive because they do not respire, but they are considered to be living organisms because they can reproduce.

## Structure of a Virus

A virus consists of two basic parts. An outer protective wall is made up of proteins called capsid, which protect the virus against harsh environments for many years. Inside this protective coat is its DNA, which reproduces with the help of the host DNA synthesis machinery.

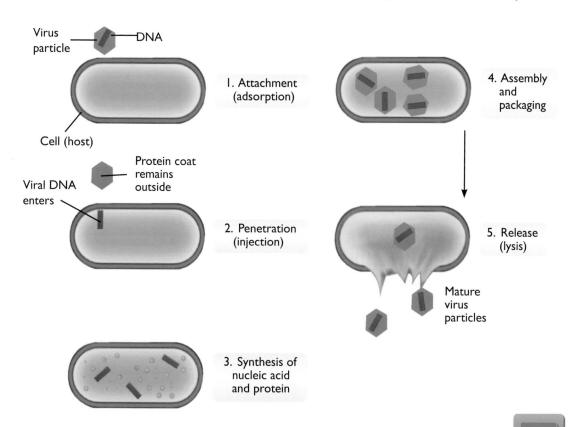

Virus particle — DNA

Cell (host)

1. Attachment (adsorption)

4. Assembly and packaging

Viral DNA enters — Protein coat remains outside

2. Penetration (injection)

5. Release (lysis)

Mature virus particles

3. Synthesis of nucleic acid and protein

# How Does a Virus Infect?

In order to grow and reproduce, viruses must enter the host cells. Once inside, they multiply in number and spread, making the host sick. Inside the host body they multiply by replicating their genetic material (DNA or RNA) with the help of the host's genetic material.

## Body's Response to Viral Infection

The immune system of our body protects us against germs. Germs generally get stuck in thick mucus or the hairy lining of the nose. Once the germs reach the organs, they cause diseases. However, in that case the body's own defensive mechanism— the immune system—is activated. In case of a strong viral attack, external help in the form of vaccines prescribed by a doctor may be required.

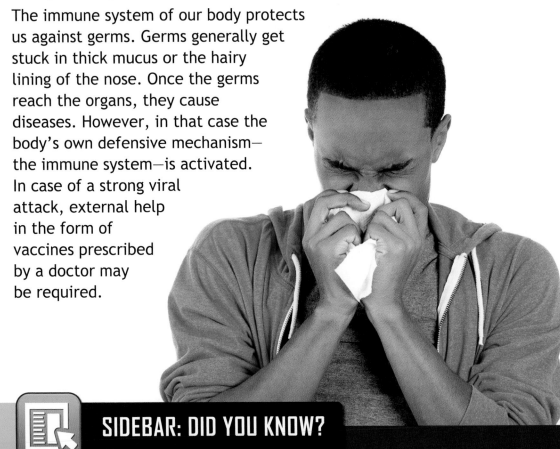

## SIDEBAR: DID YOU KNOW?

- While antibiotics can kill bacteria, they are not effective against viruses.
- Viruses can lie dormant in the body for long periods of time and may not show any symptoms of the disease.

# FUNGI

Many of us believe that mushrooms are of plant origin. However, they belong to an entirely different group called fungi. They generally appear nongreen. Some of them are very beautifully colored as they do not possess chlorophyll. Due to the lack of chlorophyll, they cannot synthesize food on their own and therefore must live as parasites or saprobes. That is why they are not grouped with plants.

## What are Fungi?

Fungi are multicelled, nonmotile plantlike organisms. They live in damp, warm places.
One type of fungus, yeast, is single-celled. Humans use yeast for producing alcohol and rising breads. They were earlier thought to be nonliving, but Louis Pasteur, a French chemist and microbiologist, discovered that yeast are living entities and cause fermentation.

 **WORDS TO UNDERSTAND**

**acetone:** a type of liquid used in paints to prevent them from becoming thick.

**microbiologist:** a person who studies microorganisms.

**nonmotile:** unable to move.

**opportunistic:** describes something that takes advantage of a particular circumstance.

# Where Do They Live?

Fungi can be found in different environments and can grow on almost anything. They may live solitarily or in mutually beneficial association with algae, or in the roots of various trees. The association between fungus and alga is known as lichen, and the association of fungal hyphae with the roots of certain trees is known as mycorrhiza (derived from the Greek words, for "mushroom" and "root"). Fungi are also seen on food, in the form of yeast or mold.

## Reproduction

Most fungi are capable of asexual and sexual reproduction. Asexual reproduction happens by fragmentation or spore formation. Some fungi release thousands of spores, which move from one place to the other by the action of wind, and after reaching on a suitable substratum, these spores can germinate and give rise to new fungi. Some of them reproduce by producing gametes in specialized areas of the hyphae called gametangia. These gametes, or sometimes even the gametangia, fuse to form a new mycelium which grows into a fungus.

## Benefits of Fungi

Fungi are economically valuable as a source of antibiotics, vitamins, and various important industry chemicals, such as alcohol, acetone and enzymes. They are extremely important in the process of soil renewal through the decomposition of organic matter. Some fungi are edible and are used to make delicious delicacies. Yeast is used to raise bread dough and in the fermentation process of beer, wine, vinegar, and cheese.

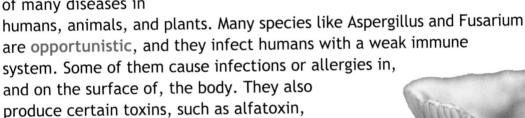

## Diseases Caused by Fungi

Fungi are considered as the causal organism of many diseases in humans, animals, and plants. Many species like Aspergillus and Fusarium are opportunistic, and they infect humans with a weak immune system. Some of them cause infections or allergies in, and on the surface of, the body. They also produce certain toxins, such as alfatoxin, which are cancerous in nature. The majority of plant diseases are also caused by fungi.

## SIDEBAR: DID YOU KNOW?

- The mushrooms on your pizza and in your salad are forms of edible fungi.
- Red squirrels gather and store dried fungi in trees and eat them in winter.

# PROTOZOA

There are two types of living organisms: prokaryotes (nucleus-less organisms) and eukaryotes (nucleus-containing organisms). Eukaryotes are further classified into two broad categories, depending upon the number of cells in the body of the organism: single-celled (unicellular) and many-celled (multicellular). Protozoa belong to the former of these classes, and constitute a group of unicellular eukaryotic organisms. The majority of protozoa are 10 to 50 micrometers (or "microns") in size.

## Reproduction

Protozoa reproduces asexually by fission, schizogony (multiple fission), and budding (pinching off a part of the parent cell). Some protozoa, however, also reproduce sexually by the fusion of gametes as in the case of plasmodium—the malaria parasite. Under certain conditions, some protozoa produce a protective form called a cyst, which enables them to survive harsh environments. Cysts also allow some pathogens to survive outside their host.

 **WORDS TO UNDERSTAND**

fission: a process in which one cell splits into two.
gastrointestinal tract: a tract including the digestive tract, beginning from the mouth and ending with the anus.
nonpathogenic: describes something that does not cause disease.
parasitic: describes an organism that benefits from living on another.

## Protozoa: Different Classes

An amoeba is the simplest of all protozoa. Amoebae can be either free-living or parasitic. Flagellates possess a trophozoite form but also possess flagella for locomotion and food-gathering. All pathogenic species are true parasites, as they are totally unable to reproduce outside the host. Ciliates have rows of hairlike cilia around their body for motility. All ciliates possess two nuclei. Some of the species form cysts. Apicomplexa lack any visible means of locomotion. They are generally intracellular parasites.

## Protozoa and Humans

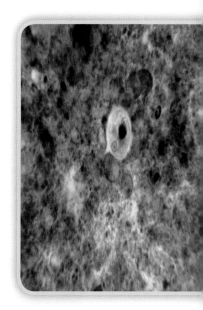

Many protozoa reside inside the gastrointestinal tract of humans. The majority of these are either nonpathogenic, or result in only mild disease. However, some of them can also cause severe disease under certain circumstances. Some protozoa that behave as human parasites can cause amebiasis, Chagas disease, cryptosporidiosis, dysentery, giardiasis, leishmaniasis, malaria, sleeping sickness, toxoplasmosis, trichomoniasis, and others. *(Some of the protozoa associated with human intestinal illness are listed in the chart on the next page.)*

## Diagnosis & Treatment of Protozoa Diseases

Most of the protozoa pathogens can be identified by a microscopic examination. For example, those of the intestine can be observed in fresh samples of the fecal material. Blood and tissue protozoa are visualized after staining. Usually, the antiprotozoal therapy is not very

| Name | Mode of Transmission | Symptoms |
|---|---|---|
| *G lamblia* | Contaminated water, fecal-oral | Nausea, bloating, gas, diarrhea, anorexia |
| *Dientamoeba fragilis* | Fecal-oral, associated with *Enterobius* | Previously thought of as commensal; may cause diarrhea, abdominal, pain, nausea |
| *Entamoeba histolytica* | Contaminated water, fecal-oral, contaminated food | Colitis, dysentery, diarrhea, liver abscess, other extraintestinal disease |
| *Cryptosporidium parvum* | Contaminated water, swimming pools, fecal-oral | Immunocompetent patients: self-limited diarrhea. Immunosuppressed patients: severe and interminable diarrhea |
| *Isospora belli* | Fecal-oral | Same as in *Cryptosporidium* |
| *Cyclospora cayetanensis* | Fecal-oral, contaminated water and food | Same as in *Cryptosporidium* |
| *Microsporidia* sp. | Fecal-oral, contaminated water | Same as in *Cryptosporidium* |
| *Balantidium coli* | Fecal-oral (frequently associated with pigs) | Colitis, diarrhea |
| *Blastocystis hominis* | Fecal-oral | May cause mild diarrhea |

effective. The treatment is hampered by the lack of effective agents for many diseases, their potential toxicity to humans, and the inability to destroy all forms of the organism. The emergence of drug resistance has also limited the therapeutic potential of many agents.

 SIDEBAR: DID YOU KNOW?

- Protozoa means "first animal." The term refers to simple eukaryotic organisms composed of a microscopic single cell.
- There are over 36,000 known species of protozoa.

# BODY DEFENSE AGAINST MICROBES

The human body is protected by a complex system of defense mechanisms that work to prevent the occurrence of disease. We have fighter cells present underneath the skin. They protect us either by preventing the entry of microbes into the body, or by killing or neutralizing the microbes inside our body. The body's first line of defense involves physical barriers such as skin, tears, cilia, saliva, and mucus.

## Skin

Skin is comprised of layers of tissue that form the natural covering of the body. Skin is made of the epidermis, dermis, and subcutaneous layers. It is waterproof, flexible, and resistant to penetration by microorganisms. Though our skin always has bacteria on it, it prevents the invasion of microorganisms unless damaged by an injury, insect bite, or burn. Only the papillomavirus can invade normal skin, causing warts. Skin also secretes certain chemicals like defensins that can kill potential invaders.

## WORDS TO UNDERSTAND

**cilia:** hairlike structures on the surface of some cells.
**defensins:** proteins that fight bacteria, fungi, and some viruses.
**organelles:** structures within cells that have particular functions.

# Mucous Membranes

These membranes line the bodily cavities and canals, and other tracts of the body such as the mouth, nose, and eyelids. They are coated with secretions that fight or trap microorganisms. For example, the mucous membranes of the eyes are bathed in tears, which contain an enzyme called lysozyme that attacks bacteria and protects the eyes from infection. The walls of the passages in the nose and airways are coated with mucus. Mucus removes the air-suspended microorganisms when we breathe—microorganisms in the air get stuck to the mucus, and are blown out of the nose.

Cilia are hairlike organelles that line the surface of certain cells and beat in rhythmic waves. Their rhythmic movement helps to move liquid past the surface of the cell. Local secretions also contain immunoglobulins, principally IgG and secretory IgA, which prevent microorganisms from attaching to host cells.

# Respiratory Tract

The respiratory tract has upper airway filters. When invading organisms reach the trachea or bronchioles, the mucociliary epithelium transports them away from the lungs. Coughing also helps remove organisms. If the organisms reach the alveoli, alveolar macrophages and tissue histiocytes engulf them. However, these defenses can be overcome by large numbers of organisms or by when their effectiveness is compromised by air pollutants.

# GI Tract

The gastrointestinal (GI) tract has a series of effective barriers, including stomach acid, pancreatic enzymes, bile, and intestinal secretions. The stomach acid (HCl) and the antibacterial activity of pancreatic enzymes, bile, and intestinal secretions help in the neutralization of microorganisms. The contractions of the intestine (peristalsis) and the normal shedding of the cells lining the intestine help remove harmful microorganisms.

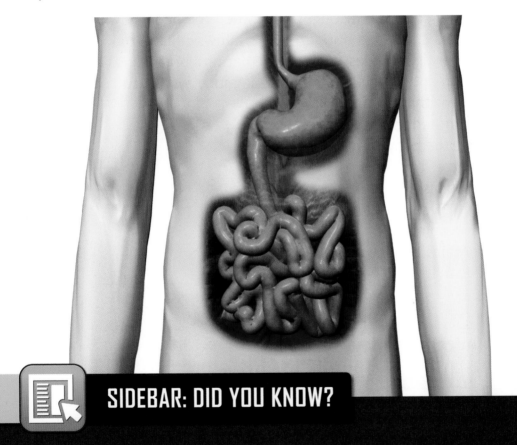

## SIDEBAR: DID YOU KNOW?

- **The skin is the thickest on the palms and soles of our feet.**
- **Your skin makes up about 15 percent of your overall body weight.**

# IMMUNE RESPONSE

When physical barriers are not able to protect the body, the second line of defense—the immune system—offers it protection against disease-causing organisms. The immune system recognizes and destroys foreign substances and organisms that enter the body.

## How Does the Immune System Work?

The immune system can distinguish between the body's own tissues and foreign substances called antigens. This allows cells of the immune system to identify and destroy only the harmful organisms. The ability to identify an antigen also permits the immune system to "remember" those antigens that the body has been exposed to in the past so that the body can mount a better and faster immune response the next time any of these antigens appear. The immune system contains billions of leukocytes that are always on guard.

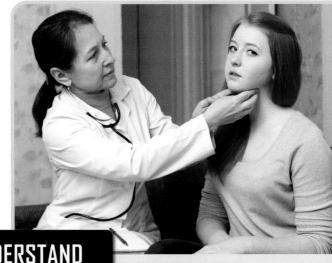

 **WORDS TO UNDERSTAND**

antigens: foreign substances that cause a response by the immune system.

capillaries: very tiny blood vessels that pass on oxygen and nutrients to cells and collect waste materials from them.

dilation: to become large.

hemoglobin: a protein in red blood cells that contain iron.

leukocyte: a white blood cell; part of the immune system.

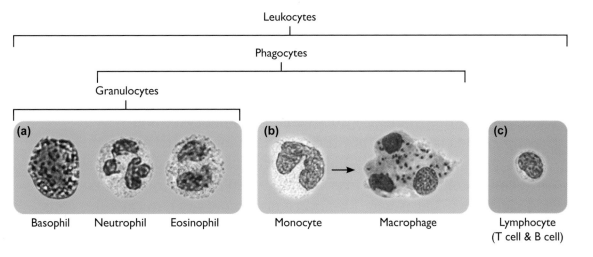

Leukocytes

Phagocytes

Granulocytes

(a)

Basophil    Neutrophil    Eosinophil

(b)

Monocyte    →    Macrophage

(c)

Lymphocyte
(T cell & B cell)

# Leukocytes

Leukocytes are present both in the blood and lymph. They are cellular components of the blood that lack hemoglobin, have a nucleus, are capable of motility, and defend the body against infection and disease. They fight with disease-causing antigens either by inflammation (or phagocytosis) or by the production of antibodies. Leukocytes are produced or stored in many locations in the body, including the thymus, spleen, and bone marrow. For this reason, they're called the lymphoid organs. These leukocytes circulate through the body between the organs and nodes through lymphatic vessels and blood vessels. The two basic types of leukocytes: phagocytes and lymphocytes.

# Phagocytes

The white blood cells that ingest the harmful bacteria, foreign particles, and dead or dying cells are called phagocytes. The most common type of phagocyte is the neutrophil, which primarily fights bacteria. Phagocytic cells eat up the foreign particle with the help of lysosomes (which secrete digestive enzymes) and break them into smaller particles. Mast cells are produced at the site of inflammation. They degranulate to produce histamine, which leads to dilation of blood capillaries.

## Lymphocytes

The two kinds of lymphocytes are B lymphocytes and T lymphocytes. Lymphocytes start out in the bone marrow. Some stay there and mature into B cells, while others leave for the thymus gland through blood, where they mature into T cells. B lymphocytes and T lymphocytes have separate functions: B lymphocytes act as the body's surveillance system—they produce antibodies to fight with antigens. T cells identify those cells that can cause tumor or cancer and kill them. That is why T cells are also known as natural killer cells. After killing the tumor or cancerous cells, they again start patrolling the blood. T cells also produce interferons, which act as antiviral compounds used to kill viruses.

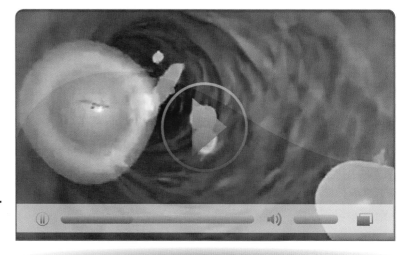

This clip shows the immune response at work.

 **SIDEBAR: DID YOU KNOW?**

- **Saliva contains antibody A, which helps to kill pathogens before they enter the stomach through the mouth.**
- **Factors such as stress and lack of sleep can impair immune system functioning.**

# INNATE & ACQUIRED IMMUNITY

The immune system can detect various agents and is able to differentiate between the healthy tissues of the body and the disease-causing agents. Immunity comprises the biological defenses of the body that protect it against infections, diseases, and those foreign substances that are likely to cause harm. There are two types of immunity: innate immunity and adaptive immunity.

## Innate Immunity

Nonspecific immunity or innate immunity is inherited at the time of birth. It includes defenses that mobilize quickly upon infection since they are produced in our body. Therefore, innate immunity is genetically determined. For example, all humans are immune to canine distemper, which is a disease common in dogs.

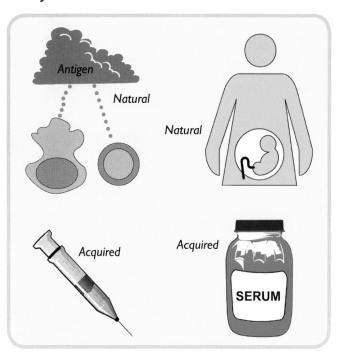

 **WORDS TO UNDERSTAND**

**innate:** describes something that a person has at birth.

**pathogen:** a disease-causing microorganism.

**proliferate:** to rapidly increase in number.

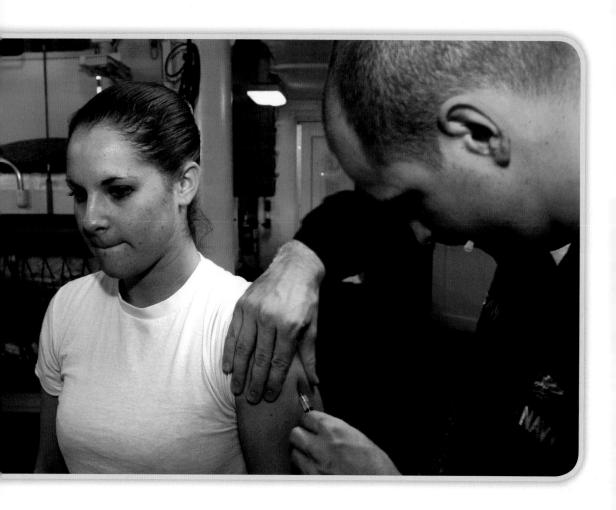

The physical barriers of our body such as skin act as a natural barrier to invading pathogens. They also secrete certain chemicals which do not allow the microorganisms to attach to the host cells, proliferate, and reproduce.

These chemicals are known as defensins and they are proteolytic (protein-breaking) polypeptides. If they enter our body, our body possesses special cells for phagocytosis (cell-eating). Two types of cells are extremely important for phagocytosis: neutrophils (smaller cells) and macrophages (larger cells). Hence, no antibodies are produced when the body uses its innate immunity. It is also called cell-mediated immunity.

# Adaptive Immunity

The second type of immunity is adaptive immunity, which is acquired after exposure to antigens. Since this immunity is attained instead of being naturally produced by the body, it is known as acquired immunity. It can also be understood as the third line of defense of the body.

*Phagocytosis and endocytosis: a phagosome or endosome containing extracellular material is formed as the cell membrane pinches together.*

It includes production of antibodies by B cells to control the proliferation and spread of antigens in the body. It is not genetically determined. For example, we suffer from measles only once in our lifetime, and then our body becomes immune to it.

We can acquire immunity either passively or actively. Active immunity is acquired by exposure to antigens either in low or high concentrations. When an antigen strikes our body or penetrates it, antibodies are produced against it. This is known as active immunity.

On the other hand, immunity acquired through vaccination or immunization is known as passive immunity. Vaccination either provides short-term immunization, as in the case of tetanus, or may benefit for the entire life as in the case of oral polio vaccine. This type of immunity which is mediated by antibodies (immunoglobulins) is also called antibody-mediated immunity or humoral immunity. Acquired immunity begins to work when innate immunity fails to prevent the invading pathogen.

 SIDEBAR: DID YOU KNOW?

- In most countries, immunization for smallpox, pertussis, diphtheria, and many other diseases is provided during childhood.

- The immune system tries to completely rid the body of those viruses and bacteria that are capable of reproducing inside it.

# LYMPHATIC SYSTEM

The lymphatic system is a circulatory drainage network that defends the body against infections or antigens by removing them from the body. It also assists in tissue repairs. If this system is blocked or there is obstruction in the flow of lymph, it can lead to edema, due to fluid retention in tissues. The lymphatic system consists of three components: vessels, fluid, and lymphoid organs.

Lymph Vessel

Lymph Node

## Vessels

A network of lymphatic vessels makes up the lymphatic system. These vessels carry lymph from the peripheral tissues to the venous system and to all the parts of the body except the central nervous system.

The smallest vessels are called lymphatic capillaries; they carry lymph to the larger

## WORDS TO UNDERSTAND

anterior: near the front.

edema: swelling.

eradicate: to remove or eliminate something completely.

lymphocytes: the cells that attack bacteria in blood.

subclavian vein: one of the two large veins on either side of the body.

lymphatic vessels and then to lymph nodes. The lymphatic vessels ultimately empty into two large collecting ducts: the thoracic duct and right lymphatic duct, which drain lymphatic fluid into the right and left subclavian vein.

## Fluid

The clear and watery fluid circulating in the lymph vessels is called lymph. It includes fluid from the intestine (chyme), which contains proteins, fats, red blood cells, white blood cells, and especially lymphocytes.

## Lymphoid Organs

Bone marrow, lymph nodes, the spleen, thymus, and tonsils are lymphoid organs. The main functions of these organs are: production of lymphocytes for destroying foreign particles, maintaining normal blood volume, and checking the distribution of various hormones.

## Bone Marrow

It is the site of the origin of pre-B and pre-T lymphocytes. In humans, the lineage of B lymphocytes can be traced to stem cells. However, in the case of birds, B cell lineage can be traced to the bursa of Fabricius.

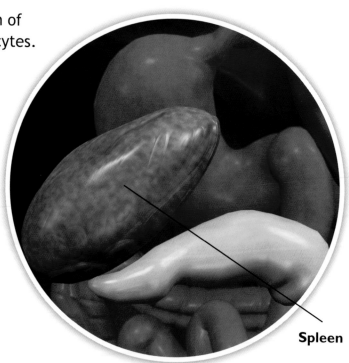

**Spleen**

## Lymph Glands

Lymph glands are small and bean-shaped, and they are also known as lymph nodes. They may become enlarged due to a tumor or infection. White blood cells are located within the lymph nodes. Their main function is filtration of fluids and immune surveillance as the immune cells are concentrated there.

## • Spleen

The spleen is located in the upper-left part of the abdomen under the ribcage, and forms a part of the lymphatic system to protect the body. It filters worn-out red blood cells and other foreign bodies from the bloodstream to help eradicate infection.

## • Thymus

The thymus is a lymphoid organ located in the upper anterior portion of the chest cavity, just behind the sternum. The hormones produced by thymus stimulate the production of certain infection-fighting cells.

**Thymus**

## • Tonsils

Tonsils are clumps of lymphoid tissue on both sides of the throat. Their main function is to defend the body by preventing the entry of nasal and oral pathogens. An infection of the tonsils is called tonsillitis.

 **SIDEBAR: DID YOU KNOW?**

- When lymphocytes fight flu- or cold-causing germs, the lymph nodes in the neck or groin, or under the arm, may swell.
- Thomas Bartholin, a Danish physician, first described the working of the lymphatic system.

# LYMPHOID CELLS

Microscopic cells called lymphoid cells are produced in the bone marrow and circulate in the blood. Finally, they enter certain organs in the human body where they differentiate, mature, and proliferate to act against antigens. They are subcategorized as: B cells, T cells, natural killer (NK) cells, and antigen-presenting cells.

## B Cells

B cells are associated with the blood vascular system, lymphatic tissues, and extracellular tissues. They are named so because they originate and mature in the bone marrow from pre-B cells. B cells are produced daily from the bone marrow, and they survive for several months. The majority of them are found in the lymph nodes, spleen, and in Peyer's patches. B cells are activated after the body's encounter with antigens. They get transformed either into plasma cells or memory cells. B cells respond to various antigens by producing different types of antibodies against them.

## WORDS TO UNDERSTAND

**cytotoxic:** toxic to living cells.

**Peyer's patches:** areas of lymphoid tissue located in the small intestine.

**proliferation:** increase of something.

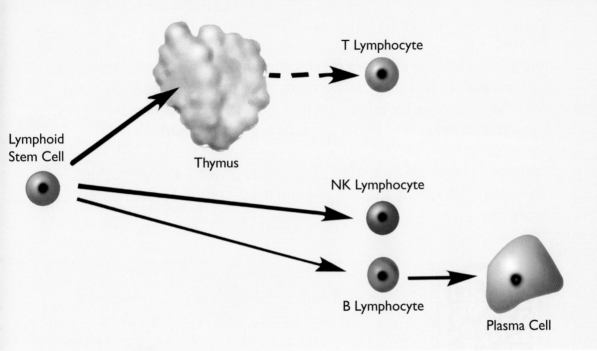

## T Cells

These are also called thymus-dependent cells. Initially they are produced from the bone marrow, but then they move to the thymus through blood where they mature. Here, they differentiate into T helper cells or cytotoxic T cells. As the name suggests, helper T cells help B cells to bind antigens and produce antibodies against them. T helper cells constitute about 95 percent of the T cells in the thymus. The remaining 5 percent are cytotoxic T cells, whose main function is to kill the antigens without the production of antibodies.

## Natural Killer (NK) Cells

NK cells are large granular lymphocytes constituting 5 to15 percent of the peripheral blood. They are also immunocompetent cells which interact with HLA cells in humans or tumor cells or virus-infected cells. Their main function is to kill the cells containing antigens. Certain classes of NK cells that possess some features of T cells release interleukins. These interleukins induce the proliferation of B cells for antibody production and also induce the aggregation of inflammatory cells.

# APCs

Antigen-presenting cells are often called APCs. These cells process an antigen into a form that can be recognized and acted upon by other cells. Various cells have been named as APCs, such as dendritic cells, Langerhan's cells, etc. Dendritic cells are star-shaped.

Lagerhan's cells are immature dendritic cells with a large nucleus. They help in trapping the antigen and presenting it to the nearest CD4 receptor.

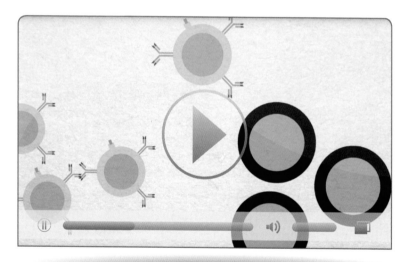

This video will tell you more about B cells.

 **SIDEBAR: DID YOU KNOW?**

- About one in 100,000 people has severe combined immunodeficiency disease, in which the immune system does not work at all.
- White blood cells make up only about one percent of our blood.

# MYELOID CELLS

The killing or neutralization of antigens in the body is mediated by myeloid cells (phagocytes). These cells possess granules in their cytoplasm; that is why they are also called granulocytes. They may possess single nucleated cells called monocytes or cells with lobed nucleus called polymorphonucleocytes or neutrophils. These granulocytes are differentiated on the basis of their staining properties.

## Neutrophils

They develop from the primary lymphoid organ—the bone marrow. Neutrophils take about two weeks to develop. They survive in the blood for 24 to 48 hours and are commonly observed in the blood smear.
In a smear, they look like round cells having a multilobed nucleus. They possess different surface receptors. Their function is to kill or neutralize antigens in blood or tissues. Their movement into tissues is called extravasation. These are the first cells to reach the site of inflammation.

## Macrophages

They are present in all organ systems and are characterized by different names in different organelles. Macrophages constitute a mononuclear phagocytic system. They are called monocytes in blood, Kupffer cells in

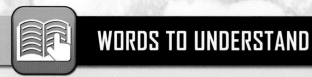

## WORDS TO UNDERSTAND

blood smear: a slide made from a drop of blood.

fibrinogen: a protein released by the liver.

permeability: an ability which allows both solid or liquid substances to pass through.

serotonin: a type of hormone that affects mood and the well being of a person.

the liver, histocytes in the connective tissue, microglial cells in the brain, and mesangial cells in kidneys. They are amoeboid-like in shape. Their main function is to heal wounds. They perform various functions, such as phagocytosis of bacterial cells and destruction of tumor cells.

## Platelets

They are also produced from megakaryocyte in the bone marrow. The normal count of platelets in humans is 150,000 to 450,000 per microliter of blood. Approximately 60 to 75 percent of the circulating platelets stay in blood and the remaining are sent to the spleen. They are actively involved in the immune response to inflammatory reactions. The platelets aggregate at the site of injury and release serotonin and fibrinogen. These chemicals increase the permeability of blood capillaries, which helps in wound healing.

## Mast Cells

These cells also originate from the bone marrow, and the mature ones circulate in the blood. Depending upon the type of tissue with which they are associated, some of them are called mucosal mast cells (associated with intestinal mucosal cells) and some are called cutaneous tissue mast cells (associated with cutaneous tissue). They contain heparin, histamine, and eosinophil chemotactic factor of anaphylaxis (ECFA).

## Eosinophil Cells

They are important clinical markers in immunodiagnosis. Their normal range is 2 to 5 percent of blood leukocytes in humans. Any increase in their range is indicative of a parasitic infection in the body. They leave the bone marrow as immature cells and enter the spleen as mature cells. They are capable of attaching, ingesting, and neutralizing the foreign antigen. These cells also induce inflammatory response.

## Basophil Cells

These immunocompetent cells are pharmacologically important. They also contain histamine and serotonin, which play an important role in providing cell-mediated immunity. They occur in small quantities, approximately 2 percent of all leukocytes. They produce inflammatory reactions for killing antigens at the site of injury.

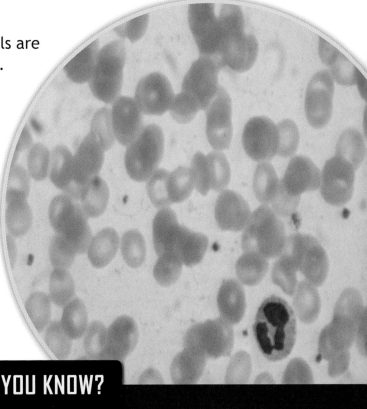

 **SIDEBAR: DID YOU KNOW?**

- Urticaria pigmentosa, a skin disease, is caused by excessive working of mast cells in infants.
- Neutrophils reach the site of injury within an hour.

# IMMUNE SYSTEM: OTHER CELLS

The cell-mediated responses of the immune system are its foremost defense against invading organisms such as bacteria, viruses, and protozoa. The immune system is made up of different types of cells. Different cells perform different functions to protect the body against a variety of ailments. However, some important immune cells have a definite role to play.

## Erythroid Progenitor Cells

Red blood cells (RBCs) originate from these progenitor cells, and they have immense physiological and immunological importance. The process of the development of RBCs in the bone marrow is called erythropoiesis. RBCs live in our body for 120 days. After that, new RBCs are generated. The average RBC count in men is roughly 4.7 million cells per micrometer and in women is 4.2 to 5.4 million cells per microliter. In 1900, Karl Landsteiner developed the concept of blood groups. In 1940, Landsteiner and Alexander Weiner discovered Rh positive and Rh negative blood groups in humans.

*Karl Landsteiner*

## WORDS TO UNDERSTAND

**benign:** not harmful.

**progenitor cell:** a descendant of the stem cell that cannot renew itself anymore.

**vertebrates:** animals with spinal cords.

# Major Histocompatibility (MHC) Molecules

MHCs play a major role in distinguishing between self- and nonself cells with the help of CD4 and CD8 cells. They are basically a cluster of genes found on the short arm of human chromosome 6. They are present on the surface of the cells responsible for lymphocyte recognition and antigen presentation. MHCs are also referred to as human leukocyte antigen (HLA) in the case of humans.

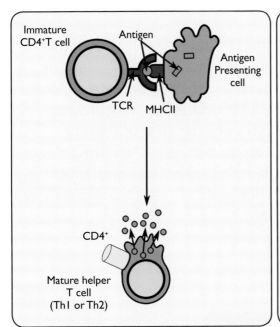
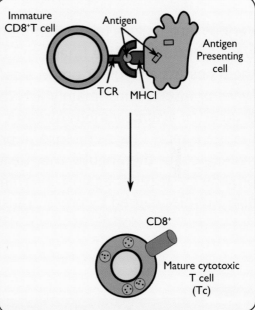

# Complement Proteins

Complement proteins are a complex group of serum proteins, which constitute about 10 percent of the serum proteins and glycoprotein in humans and other **vertebrates**. They are enzymatic, thus they kill invading organisms.

Complement proteins produce a cascade reaction–like chain reaction, in which the first enzyme upon activation catalyzes the second enzyme, and so on. This induces a series of inflammatory responses, which helps to fight infections. The antigen and antigen-bearing cells are killed by the complement pathway.

# Cytokines (Interleukins)

Lymphocytes and other cells of the immune system secrete certain glycoprotein molecules in response to the appropriate stimulus or infection. These glycoproteins are called interleukins or cytokines. They are produced on their own in response to immune stimulus. They can be autocrine (act on cells that secrete them) or paracrine (act on nearby cells) or endocrine (act on distant cells) in their function. They promote cellular growth of the components of the immune system.

Various interleukins have been identified to date. The first cytokine was identified by Alice Isaacs and team Lindemann in 1957. Many of them possess antitumor properties. Macrophages also secrete various types of interleukins (mainly IL1, IL6, IL12, and TNF). They provide protection against various diseases such as bacterial septic shock, benign tumor, Chagas disease (a protozoan disease). They are potential molecules for therapeutic use. Certain interleukins are safe, which provide great relief against inflammation, cancer, infectious diseases, and allergies caused by organ transplant.

## SIDEBAR: DID YOU KNOW?

- RBCs comprise about 44 percent of your blood.
- It takes between 20 to 60 seconds for an RBC to travel around the body.

# HUMAN BLOOD GROUPS

Blood is an important component of our body that serves many functions. It consists of many types of cells floating around in the plasma fluid. Red blood cells (RBCs) contain hemoglobin. Therefore, RBCs are responsible for transporting oxygen to, and removing carbon dioxide from, the body tissues. White blood cells (WBCs) fight infection, whereas platelets help the blood to clot.

## Blood Groups

Differences in our blood groups are due to the presence or absence of some protein molecules called antigens and antibodies. The antigens are located on the surface of RBCs and the antibodies are in the blood plasma. Different individuals have different types and combinations of these proteins. The blood type depends on the genes that have been inherited from parents.

 **WORDS TO UNDERSTAND**

**alleles:** an alternate form of gene.

**hemoglobin:** a protein that binds oxygen.

**universal donor:** someone whose blood can be transfused into anyone else.

**universal recipient:** someone who can take a blood transfusion from any blood type.

## How to Know Your Blood Group?

If the blood group is A, there are A antigens on the surface of RBCs and B antibodies in the blood plasma. If the blood group is B, RBCs' surfaces have B antigens and the plasma contains A antibodies. In the case of the AB blood group, both A and B antigens are present on the surface of the RBCs and no (A or B) antibodies are present in the blood plasma. If the blood group is O, neither A or B antigens are present on the surface of the RBCs, but both A and B antibodies are present in the blood plasma.

## Rh Factor

There is one more antigen on RBCs' surface that is not present in all individuals. It is called the Rh factor. Those who have it belong to Rh+ blood group, and those who lack it belong to Rh- blood group. Hence, if the RBCs possess antigen A on their surface, antibody B in the blood plasma and also the Rh factor, the blood group will be designated as A Rh+. And if the RBCs possess antigen A and B on their surface and no antibodies in the blood plasma, with the Rh factor also absent, the blood group will be designated AB Rh-.

## Inheritance of Blood Groups

The inheritance is controlled by three alleles: A, B, and O. Where A and B are codominant, O is recessive to both of these. Hence, O blood group will be present when both alleles A and B are absent, and the individual will have a genotype OO. On the other hand, when both A and B alleles are present, the blood group will neither be A nor B, but AB.

## Blood Transfusions

Mixing the blood of two individuals can lead to blood clumping. The clumped red cells can cause toxic reactions and even fatal consequences. These clumps are formed due to the reaction between antigens and antibodies. Those with blood group AB are universal recipients, whereas individuals with blood group O are universal donors.

 SIDEBAR: DID YOU KNOW?

- ABO blood groups are inherited through genes present on chromosome 9.
- The father of human blood groups—Karl Landsteiner—made it possible to determine ABO blood groups. He was awarded the Nobel Prize (1930) for this discovery.

# ALLERGY

An allergy (hypersensitivity reaction) is a type of inflammatory response with **deleterious** effects leading to significant tissue damage and may even cause death in extreme cases. An allergy is a reaction of the immune system to something which the body doesn't accept. People who have allergies are often sensitive to various substances that are likely to cause allergic reactions, such as pollen, spores, dust, food, medicines, and insect stings.

## How Do We Get Allergies?

Our immune system protects us from the invading organisms that can cause illness. In the case of allergy, your immune system mistakes an otherwise harmless substance as an invader. The immune system

## WORDS TO UNDERSTAND

**ailment:** a medical condition or disease.
**deleterious:** harmful.
**immunoglobulin:** a Y-shaped antibody produced by B cells.

overreacts to the allergen by producing immunoglobulin E (IgE). These antibodies travel to cells that release histamine and other chemicals, causing an allergic reaction. Allergy is a hereditary ailment. It usually begins to develop in childhood, although it can show up at any age.

## Symptoms

An allergic reaction typically triggers symptoms like runny nose, sneezing, itching, rashes, swelling, or asthma. Allergies can make you feel very uncomfortable. A severe reaction, called anaphylaxis, is life-threatening.

## Common Allergies

Dust allergy: Sneezing is not always the symptom of the cold. Sometimes, it is an allergic reaction to dust particles in the air. These allergens may give rise to allergic symptoms. Medically, it is known as Allergic Rhinitis. It is also called Hay fever. Allergic rhinitis is an inflammation or irritation of the mucous membrane that lines the nose. It is one of the common diseases seen in all age groups.

Pollen allergy: During spring and summer, tiny particles known as pollen are released from trees, weeds, and grasses. Although their mission is reproduction, many are never able to do so. Instead, they enter human noses and throats, triggering a type of seasonal allergic rhinitis called pollen allergy. The symptoms of this allergy usually depend on the season in which it occurs. Many of the foods, drugs, or animals that cause or carry allergies can be avoided to a great extent, but there is no easy way to evade pollen.

## Precautions

It is more difficult to avoid dust and mold. Though it is impractical to create an "allergy-proof" home, at least the bedroom should be made as allergen-free as possible. Move out all unnecessary furniture, books and other waste things from your home. Clean the curtains, beds, and carpets frequently. Keep your home atmosphere clean and free from dust and mold. Avoid "allergic foods" and maintain a balanced diet. Sleep with your head elevated to prevent nasal congestion during the night. Drink adequate fluids to loosen the secretions in your nose and throat. Exercise regularly.

 **SIDEBAR: DID YOU KNOW?**

- Allergies affect around 50 million people in the United States.
- Anti-allergy medicines block histamines from attaching to their receptors. That is why they relieve allergy symptoms and are called antihistamines.

# INFLAMMATION

A mosquito bite can sometimes result in redness, swelling and pain. This redness along with the swelling and pain is known as inflammation. Hence, inflammation is the response of the tissues to irritations or pathogen infection or injury. It is a protective mechanism of the body to trap an antigen at the site of infection. The body tries to eliminate pathogens from tissues and intracellular spaces by trapping antigens. Depending on the type of injury, inflammation can be of two types.

## Acute Inflammation

It develops within a few hours of infection. Sometimes it can occur within seconds or minutes. It is characterized by five mediators: heat, redness, swelling, pain, and loss of function. Inflammation is actually the aggregation of inflammatory cells, such as lymphocytes, leukocytes, B cells, T cells, macrophages, monocytes, neutrophils, and platelets. Immediately after the injury,

## WORDS TO UNDERSTAND

cardiovascular: related to the heart and blood vessels.

constriction: to contract.

intracellular: occurring within a cell or cells.

lacrimation: the flow of tears.

there is constriction of arterioles and dilation of small blood vessels, which increase the permeability and the protein-rich plasma exudes into the extra cellular fluids, thus inducing inflammation.

## Chronic Inflammation

Certain microparasites such as viruses, bacteria, protozoa, and fungi, and certain macroparasites such as trematodes, cestodes, and nematodes evade immune responses of the host and are able to persist in the host for longer time periods. The long period of exposure or frequent exposure to pathogens induces chronic inflammation.

Chronic inflammation can cause cardiovascular diseases. When the blood vessels are blocked by low-density lipoprotein (LDL or "bad" cholesterol), the white blood cells of the immune system move to the arteries and settle in the artery wall. Once there, they eat up the "bad" cholesterol, which causes damage to the arteries and increases the chances of heart attack.

## Mechanism of Inflammation

Inflammation is the result of degranulation of mast cells. Mast cells secrete histamine and serotonin. The secretion of histamine is mediated by sodium ions.

Histamines affect blood vessels and smooth muscles and exocrine glands. They dilate blood vessels and increase vascular permeability. It also causes the synthesis of selectin in vessels, which can lead to the rolling of neutrophils.

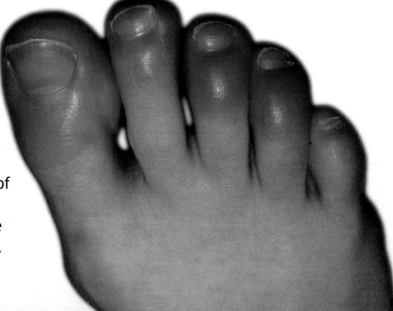

Histamine also induces contractions of the smooth muscles of the GI tract, salivation, lacrimation, and bronchial mucus secretion.

Serotonin causes contraction of blood vessels but has little effect on vascular permeability. Phospholipase breaks down the membrane of monocytes, neutrophils, and macrophages into fatty acids during cellular damage. These fatty acids are transformed into leukotrienes or prostaglandins. Both of these play an important role in inflammation.

## Controlling Inflammation

It is not every time that a mosquito and you get an inflammation. Some inflammation may not occur since plasma contains various factors that inactivate the components causing inflammation. When these plasma factors are unable to deactivate the inflammation-causing cells, the symptoms of inflammation may begin to show.

## SIDEBAR: DID YOU KNOW?

- Anti-inflammatory foods are rich in antioxidants that help control chronic inflammation.
- Anti-inflammatory foods may also help prevent heart attacks.

# ANTIBODY

Antibodies are the glycoprotein particles designed to provide immunity or protection to the host against infectious organisms. Antibodies can identify the proteins called antigens present on the infectious molecule as nonself and induce a reaction inside the body against them. They constitute a part of humoral immunity or antibody-mediated immunity or B cell-induced immunity. Antibodies are produced by B cells. They occur in many body fluids, such as tears, mucus, saliva, urine, and milk, and in the fluids in respiratory and uterine tracts. Antibodies are of five types.

## IgG

Immunoglobulin G (IgG) or gamma globulin is the most abundant class of antibodies, constituting 80 percent of the total immunoglobulins.

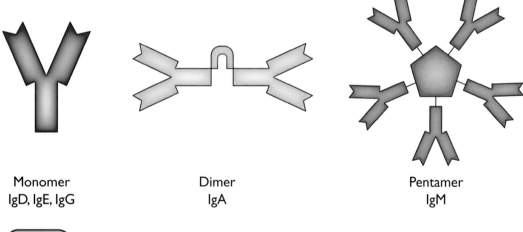

| Monomer | Dimer | Pentamer |
|:---:|:---:|:---:|
| IgD, IgE, IgG | IgA | IgM |

 **WORDS TO UNDERSTAND**

abundant: plentiful.

cholera: a bacterial disease of the intestine.

humoral: relating to bodily fluids, especially in the immune system.

IgG is found in mother's milk during the first few weeks and provides innate immunity to the baby. It helps in fighting infections and diseases. Donated human blood is used to make immunoglobulin injections, which are used to treat conditions that weaken the immune system.

## IgM

Immunoglobulin M (IgM) is found in the serum. It is the largest antibody in the human circulatory system, also known as macromolecular antibody owing to its high molecular weight. It remains in the blood and defends the body against infectious agents that enter the blood. Due to its large size, IgM cannot diffuse out from blood vessels. Therefore, very low quantities of IgM are found in interstitium. In a newborn, the detection of IgM is an indicator of infections such as syphilis, rubella, or toxoplasmosis.

## IgA

Immunoglobulin A (IgA) is found in external secretions like milk, saliva, tears, and mucus. It acts as a nonsticky cover over the intestinal epithelial cells, thus preventing a large number of antigens from crossing

the epithelium and entering the intestine. This antibody provides protection against many bacterial diseases, such as cholera caused by vibrio cholerae.

## IgD

Immunoglobulin D (IgD) has a four polypeptide chain structure. This antibody is generally susceptible to proteolytic digestion and has very short half-life.

This is because their hinge region is exposed. IgDs are active against penicillin, insulin, diphtheria, toxoid and thyroid tissues, and nuclear antigens. They generally act as B cell receptors.

## IgE

Immunoglobulin E (IgE) is present in very low concentrations in body fluids. It does not have a hinge region. It plays a very important role in type-1 hypersensitivity reactions and allergic manifestations. This antibody has epsilon heavy chain and this epsilon is very susceptible to receptors on mast cells and basophils. It causes degranulation of mast cells which release certain vasoactive amines, such as histamines, cytokines, and other inflammatory components responsible for fever and asthma. The main function of IgE is to provide immunity against parasites, such as parasitic worms.

**Find out more about Ig antibodies.**

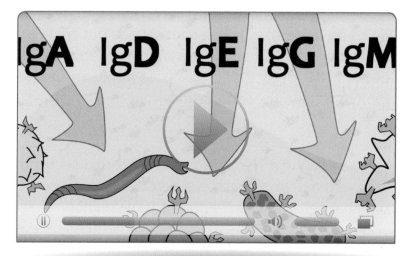

# ANTIGEN

All germs possess certain proteins on their surface which induce immune response in our body. Antigens (proteins)— present around viruses or protozoan parasites, enter into the host body and induce the generation of an immune response by the formation of antibodies. Antigens possess special motifs called antigenic determinants, which induce an immune response in the host. The capacity of an antigen to produce an immune response is called antigenicity. Though usually foreign particles contain antigens, sometimes the inner cells of our body become antigenic (nonself) and produce antibodies against it. Antigens contain specific sites to which the antibodies bind. These sites are called antigenic determinants or epitopes and the corresponding sites in antibodies are called paratopes. The strength of binding an antigen and antibody depends upon the forces of attraction between the two.

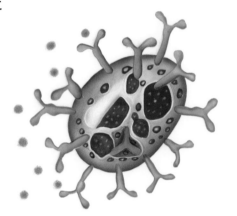

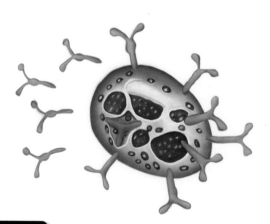

 **WORDS TO UNDERSTAND**

epitope: the part of an antigen molecule where an antibody attaches.

immunosuppressed: describes someone whose immune system is weakened.

paratope: the part of an antibody that recognizes an antigen.

## Composition

An Antigen can be a living or nonliving entity and may be a protein, a polysaccharide, an amino acid or a carbohydrate. In the case of bacteria, an antigen is always a carbohydrate, whereas in all other cases, it is a protein in nature.

## Antigen Recognition by B Cells

Each B cell has many thousands of B cell receptors (BCR). BCRs help in the recognition of an antigen on the surface of B cells, which will then differentiate into plasma cells and memory cells. Plasma cells secrete certain antibodies. Sometimes plasma cells become cancerous; these cancerous cells are called myelomas. Myeloma proteins can be present in any part of the body. For instance, if they are present in large numbers in bones, they cause multiple fractures because of the destruction of osteocytes. If a large number of myeloma proteins are present in blood, it can cause heart failure. Patients with myeloma proteins are highly immunosuppressed.

## Antigen Recognition by T-Cells

T cells recognize antigens with the help of their T cell receptors called TCR. TCRs are present on the surface of T lymphocytes. Each receptor has an extracellular domain, a transmembrane domain, and an intracellular domain. Different TCRs are represented by different gene rearrangements. In this case, antigen recognition is assisted by various accessory molecules like CD3 antigen receptor, zeta, and eta chains. Unlike B cells which can bind a wide range of antigens through its antibodies, T cells govern both humoral and cellular immunity tissues. As soon as an antigen binds with TCR, a signal is transmitted to transacting chains, which triggers the activation of phospholipase C and other factors. These factors are responsible for the induction of T cell-mediated cellular response. They lead to phagocytosis of an antigen, or T helper cells provide this antigen to B cells to produce antibodies to neutralize antigens.

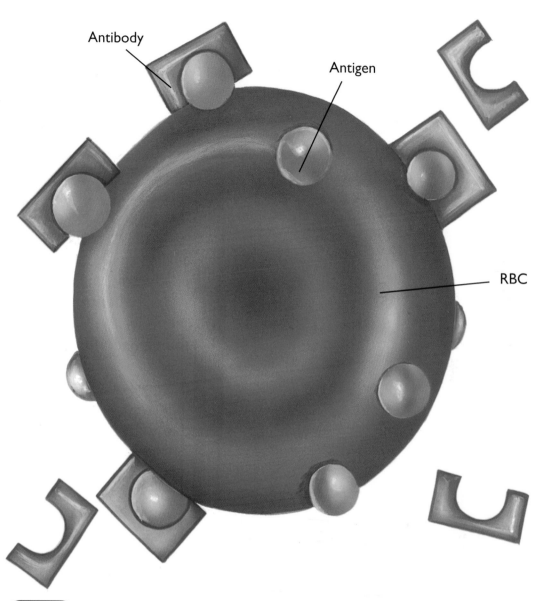

Antibody

Antigen

RBC

# IMMUNODEFICIENCY DISEASES

Our internal defense system is able to differentiate between self- and nonself cells and is able to kill the **alien** cells. For this purpose, we have three different lines of defense: the skin as the first line, the second line mediated by B cells, and the third mediated by T cells. If

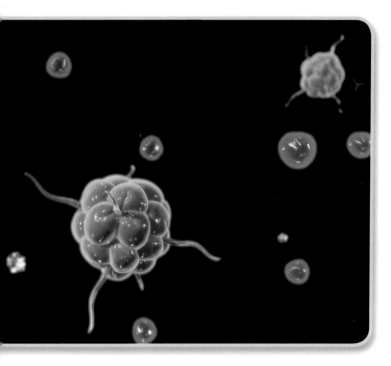

the defense cells of the body fail to recognize antigens or are deficient in any way, the immune system will not work properly, thereby leading to immunodeficiency syndromes. These diseases may be inherited or may arise due to the combined deficiency of several immune system components. There are four types of immunodeficiency syndromes.

 **WORDS TO UNDERSTAND**

**alien:** here, foreign to the body.

**congenital:** something that a person suffers from since birth, for example, congenital heart disease.

**hypothyroidism:** a condition in which the thyroid gland does not function correctly.

# Primary Immunodeficiency Diseases

These are inherited diseases, generally referred to as genetic diseases. They affect both humans and animals. The inherited defects may lead to natural immunity diseases, stem cell deficiency diseases as well as B and T cell deficiency diseases. Stem cells are the progenitors of all lymphocytes and other blood components. B cell deficiency leads to various diseases like Bruton's or congenital agammaglobulinemia. Similarly, hypothyroidism is caused by the deficiency of T cells.

IgA deficiency is the most common immunodeficiency disorder. IgA is an immunoglobulin found primarily in the saliva and other body fluids that help guard the entrances to the body. IgA deficiency is a disorder in which the body doesn't produce enough of the IgA antibody. Those with this deficiency tend to have allergies or get more cold and other respiratory infections, but the condition is usually not severe.

## CID and SCID

These are the most serious disorders caused by the defective functioning of T and B cells. An enzyme—recombinase—is responsible for causing these diseases. In the absence of this enzyme, T and B cells are produced without their receptors. One of the most important combined immunodeficiency diseases (CID) is adenosine deaminase (ADA). This disease is caused by the deficiency of adenosine deaminase enzyme, which is required to convert adenosine and deoxyadenosine to inosine and deoxyinosine for the synthesis of DNA.

In persons suffering from these diseases, the purine metabolites are accumulated, which leads to the killing of T cells, and thus results in the loss of cell-mediated immunity. Severe combined immunodeficiency (SCID) is caused due to a defect in hematopoietic stem cells or defective development of lymphoid organs.

## Secondary Immunodeficiency Diseases

These diseases are the consequences of malnutrition, excessive exercise, drugs, trauma, pollution, and parasitic infections due to heavy metal toxicity. All these factors result in a reduced number of lymphocytes. In the case of traumas like burns, accidents, and injuries, patients often die from sepsis due to immunodeficiency.

## Acquired Immunodeficiency Syndrome (AIDS)

The causes of AIDS are well known now. It is caused by HIV which fails the immune system of humans leading to various infectious diseases. Patients suffering from HIV can experience high temperature, weight loss, headache, and diarrhea, among other symptoms.

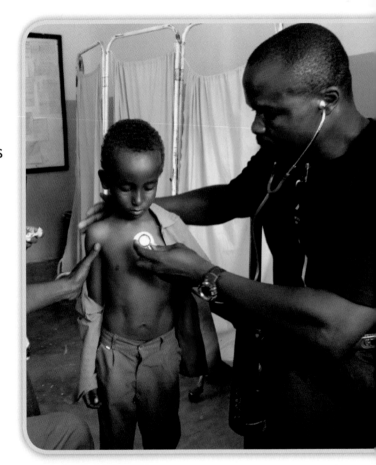

## SIDEBAR: DID YOU KNOW?

- Deficiency of B cells causes frequent bacterial infections, while deficiency of T cells causes viral infections.
- Infants suffering from SCID generally have skin diseases, diarrhea, pneumonia, mouth rashes, and throat infections.

# AUTOIMMUNE DISEASES

Our immune system protects us against different diseases and infections. However, sometimes the immune system mistakenly attacks the healthy cells in the body. This is how autoimmune diseases are caused. It can be said that autoimmune diseases are those which are caused by immune cells as they are not able to differentiate between self and nonself cells and start killing self cells instead of nonself cells. Hence, these diseases are very dangerous.

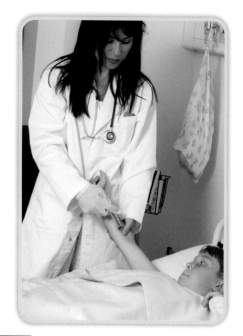

It has not been established what causes the immune system to fail to discriminate between healthy cells and antigens. However, it is argued that certain microorganisms and drugs are capable of triggering such changes. Alzheimer's disease, cancer, heart disease, and strokes are caused when the immune system fails to function properly.

 ## WORDS TO UNDERSTAND

Alzheimer's disease: a disease that causes increasing problems with memory and thought.

local: here, refers to disease that only impact a specific part of the body.

systemic: here, refers to diseases that damage numerous parts of the body.

# Types of Autoimmune Diseases

They are of two types of autoimmune diseases: systemic and local. The diseases are categorized according to the affected organ. Generally, in all autoimmune diseases fatigue, low grade fever, and dizziness are some common symptoms. They can be diagnosed by simple laboratory tests.

# What Causes Autoimmune Diseases?

Though there is a lack of clarity on why our own defensive cells (antibodies) become autoantibodies, certain experimental evidence says that there are certain privileged locations in our body where immune reactions do not take place. For example, in our brain there is no antigen-antibody interaction despite the presence of certain antigens. If the brain suffers from an injury caused by an accident, these antigens are released into the blood and they provoke an immune response which produces B and T cells to attain tolerance. These hidden antigens sometimes induce autoimmune disorders in our body. Sometimes some genetic factors induce these diseases. In other cases, oversecretion of certain hormones may lead to autoimmune diseases.

## Women are More Susceptible

Some research shows that women are more susceptible to autoimmune disorders than men since they have stronger inflammatory responses when their immune system is triggered as compared to men. Another theory believes that the hormonal difference between men and women is the reason behind the vulnerability of women to autoimmune disorders. Fluctuations in female hormones during conditions such as pregnancy, menstrual cycles, and others cause a flaring up of autoimmune diseases. This indicates that sex hormones have a role to play in autoimmune disorders.

 **SIDEBAR: DID YOU KNOW?**

- Nearly one in five Americans suffers from autoimmune diseases.
- Blood vessels, connective tissues, joints, muscles, red blood cells, and the skin are some organs and tissues commonly affected by autoimmune diseases.

# INFECTIONS AND INFECTIOUS DISEASES

Communicable or transmissible diseases are caused by microorganisms such as bacteria or fungi, viruses, or parasites and are transmitted from one person to another. These can be spread through direct contact or air, depending on the pathogen. Numerous viruses, bacteria, and fungi are capable of causing diseases. They can directly invade the defenses of the host and cause disease, or an infectious disease can develop as a result of complications.

## Some Infectious Diseases

**Eye Infection:** When bacteria cause an eye infection, the eye drains a yellow discharge (pus). This condition is also called bacterial conjunctivitis, runny eyes, or watery eyes. Symptoms include yellow discharge in the eye, eyelids stuck together with pus, especially after sleeping, redness in the sclera, and puffy eyelids.

 **WORDS TO UNDERSTAND**

**anemia:** a condition that's caused by a lack of red blood cells.
**communicable:** infectious.
**sclera:** the white part of the eyeball.

**Hepatitis:** a viral infection, in which the liver gets inflamed. Skin discoloration (yellowing) and discharge of dark urine are some common symptoms of hepatitis. Nausea and loss of appetite are also some symptoms seen when one contracts hepatitis. Hepatitis viruses are of five types: A, B, C, D, and E.

**Pneumonia:** a lung infection characterized by inflammation and is often the result of a bacterial or viral infection. Problems in breathing, chest pain, and fever are some common symptoms. Blood tests and chest X-rays are the diagnostic tools used to confirm the condition of pneumonia.

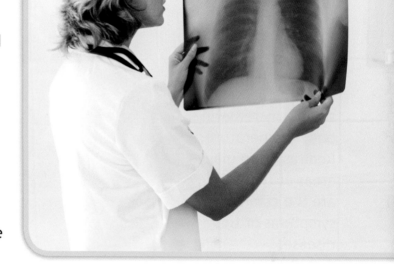

**Tuberculosis (TB):** a bacterial infection of the lungs is usually accompanied by excessive and prolonged coughing that produces blood. The disease is noticed in the advanced stages.
It is an airborne infection; TB can affect anyone irrespective of age.

**Oral thrush:** a fungal infection that is the result of overgrowth of fungus in the lining of the mouth. It leads to an uncomfortable feeling inside the mouth and is characterized by the presence of white lesions on the tongue. In severe cases, these open wounds are also seen on the gums and the tonsils. Oral thrush is frequently diagnosed in infants, but in most cases it is a minor issue.

**Malaria:** a parasitic infection that is contracted through mosquito bites. In other words, the mode of transmission is contact with mosquitoes. High fever, excessive sweating, anemia, and blood in stools, are the main symptoms of this disease. A patient of malaria also exhibits flu-like symptoms.

**Dengue fever:** This is another viral infection caused by mosquito bites. The virus gets transmitted into the body when the mosquito bites the victim. The viral infection causes a sudden increase in body temperature. Red rashes in many areas of the skin are the commonest symptoms of this disease.

## SIDEBAR: DID YOU KNOW?

- Malaria is caused by the bite of a female anopheles mosquito, since it is the vector of the malarial protozoan.
- Dengue is caused by the bite of mosquito Aedes aegypti.

# AIDS

Acquired immunodeficiency syndrome (AIDS) is the final stage of HIV, which causes severe damage to the immune system. HIV stands for human immunodeficiency virus. It is one of a group of viruses which have single-stranded RNA as their genetic material, and are hence known as retroviruses. After getting into body, HIV kills or damages the cells of the immune system. The body tries to keep up by making new cells or trying to kill the virus. Over a period of time, HIV destroys the body's ability to fight infections and certain cancers. Its symptoms start appearing when a virus has destroyed the body's defenses to the extent that the immune cell count falls to a critical level. This makes the person highly susceptible to various infections and diseases.

 **WORDS TO UNDERSTAND**

**facilitate:** to make something easier or more likely.
**prolonged:** extended.
**susceptible:** vulnerable to something.

# Transmission of AIDS

HIV can be transmitted from an infected person to a healthy person by blood transfusions, vaginal secretions, or through semen. HIV transmission can occur through unprotected sexual contact, from pregnant mother to her baby (before or during birth), or by direct blood contact (through blood transfusions or injecting drugs with needles). It is important to note that AIDS is not a communicable disease and the virus does not spread by casual contact such as shaking hands, or sharing things with an infected person. HIV is also unlikely to be spread through certain body fluids such as saliva, tears, sweat, feces, or urine unless it is contaminated with infected blood.

## Symptoms

HIV-infected people may not know that they are suffering from it right away. The symptoms are sometimes not seen for years and the only way to find out whether one is infected or not is by taking a blood test. Symptoms can be categorized into early and late.

**Early symptoms:** In the early stages of HIV, there are a few symptoms such as headache, fever, tiredness, and enlarged lymph nodes in the neck and groin area. These symptoms usually disappear within a week or so and can be mistaken for other viral infections such as the flu.

**Late symptoms:** During the later stages of HIV infection, the virus severely weakens the immune system and infected people suffer from rapid weight loss, pneumonia, sores of the mouth, anus, and genital areas, extreme and unexplained tiredness, diarrhea that can last for over a week, recurring fever, and profuse night sweats along with prolonged swelling of lymph glands in the armpits, neck, and groin, and finally, memory loss and depression. Each of these symptoms can be related to other illnesses.

## Prevention

In spite of so many medical efforts, there is no effective vaccine for HIV. The only way to prevent infection by the virus is to avoid behaviors that put you at risk, such as sharing needles or having unprotected sex. Hence, one must be cautious to avoid activities that facilitate the contraction of HIV.

 **SIDEBAR: DID YOU KNOW?**

- At the end of 2016, there were more than 36 million people living with HIV worldwide.

- More than a million Americans are living with HIV; as many as one in eight may not know they have it.

# VACCINES AND VACCINATION

A vaccine is a biological preparation that improves immunity to a particular disease. A vaccine typically contains an agent that resembles a disease-causing microorganism, and is often made from weakened or killed forms of the disease-causing microbe, its toxins, or one of its surface proteins. Vaccines stimulate the body's immune system to recognize the agent as foreign, destroy it, and "remember" it, so that the immune system can easily recognize and destroy any of these microorganisms when it encounters them later.

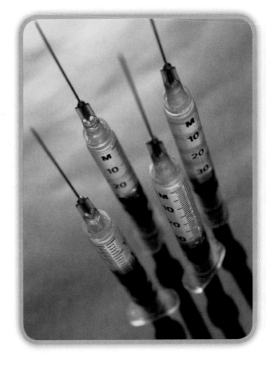

## What is Vaccination?

Vaccination is the administration of antigenic material (vaccines) to stimulate the immune system of an individual to develop adaptive immunity to a disease. Vaccination can prevent the effects of infection caused by many pathogens. The primary goal

 **WORDS TO UNDERSTAND**

attenuated: weakened.

recombinant: relating to genetically engineered DNA.

toxin: any harmful or poisonous substance that can cause diseases and infections.

of vaccination is to provide immunity by inducing a memory response to an infectious microorganism using a nontoxic antigen preparation. It is important to produce the appropriate immunity—antibody and/or cellular immunity. There are various types of vaccines, including live **attenuated** vaccines, inactivated vaccines, and others.

## Live Attenuated Vaccines

Live attenuated vaccines contain a version of the living microbe that has been weakened in the lab so that it can't cause disease. They elicit strong cellular and antibody responses and often confer lifelong immunity with only one or two doses. However, live attenuated vaccines are not safe for everyone. Those with damaged or weakened immune systems (due to medical conditions, such as HIV) cannot be given live vaccines. Another limitation of live attenuated vaccines is that they need to be refrigerated so that they can stay potent.

## Inactivated Vaccines

Inactivated vaccines are produced by killing the disease-causing microbe with chemicals, heat, or radiation. Such vaccines are more stable and safer than live vaccines since the dead microbes can't mutate back to their disease-causing state. Inactivated vaccines usually don't require refrigeration and can be easily stored and transported in a freeze-dried form. Most inactivated vaccines, however, stimulate a weaker immune system response as compared to live vaccines. Hence, it takes several additional doses of inactivated vaccines, called booster shots, to maintain one's immunity.

## Toxoid Vaccines

These vaccines are used when a bacterial toxin is the main cause of illness. Inactivated toxins are treated with formalin, a solution of formaldehyde and sterilized water to make these vaccines. Such "detoxified" toxins, called toxoids, are safe for use in vaccines. When the immune system receives a vaccine containing a harmless toxoid, it learns how to fight off the natural toxin. Vaccines against diphtheria and tetanus are examples of toxoid vaccines.

## DNA Vaccines

DNA vaccines are made of genetically engineered DNA that stimulates an immunological response. Intramuscular injections of circular DNA results in DNA uptake by muscle cells, expression of the encoded protein, and induction of both humoral and cell-mediated immunity.

## Recombinant Vaccines

Using molecular genetics, selective recombinant proteins of defined epitopes can be prepared that protect the host. This approach overcomes the problem of disease complication which might occur due to the use of modified live vaccines.

**Find out more about how vaccines work.**

## SIDEBAR: DID YOU KNOW?

- Edward Jenner developed the vaccine for smallpox in 1796.
- Vaccines prevent an estimated 2.5 million deaths every year.

# TEXT-DEPENDENT QUESTIONS

1.  How do germs cause diseases?

2.  How are fungi used to benefit humans?

3.  What are the major components of the lymphatic system?

4.  What is acquired immunity?

5.  What is inflammation and how does the body use inflammation to protect itself?

6.  What are some common allergies?

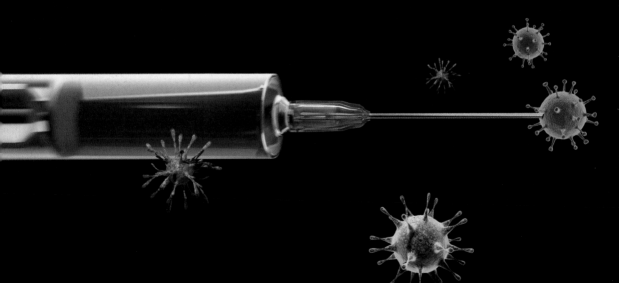

7.  What are autoimmune disorders?

8.  Give three examples of infectious diseases.

9.  About how many Americans have the HIV virus?

10. Why is vaccination important?

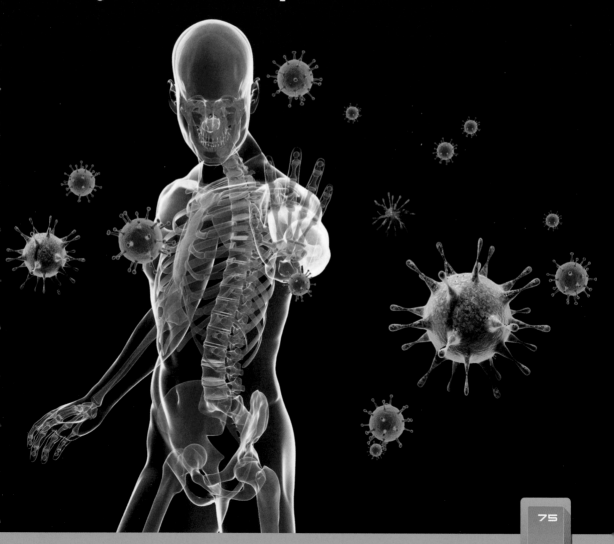

1. Find a diagram of the human body online and print it out. Using this text and other sources, label the major components of the lymphatic system. Be sure to include the tonsils, thymus, spleen, and lymph nodes in your diagram.

2. Find out more about the life and work of one of the scientists mentioned in this text: Alexander Fleming (penicillin); Thomas Bartholin (lymphatic system); Karl Landsteiner (blood groups); Edward Jenner (vaccines). Write a short report about him. How did his discovery come about? How did his work change the world?

3. Research tips on how to prevent spreading illnesses such as colds and the flu. Make a list of those tips and then turn it into a poster to educate people on how to keep themselves and others healthier.

4. Find out more about groups that work to prevent AIDS transmission, either in the United States or in other countries. What strategies do they use to educate the public about how to keep themselves safe? Which strategies have been more or less effective?

5. Find out more about polio. Here are some questions to get you started: What sort of disease is it and how did the disease affect children? Why were parents so afraid of it? Who invented the vaccine? How many people contract polio today versus before the vaccine?

# FURTHER READING

Caravan, Thomas. *Fighting Illness and Injury: The Immune System.*
Logan, IA: PowerKids Press, 2015.

Carver, Catherine. *Immune: How Your Body Defends and Protects You.*
New York: Bloomsbury, 2017.

Gardy, Jennifer. *It's Catching: The Infectious World of Germs.*
Berkeley, CA: OwlKids Books, 2014.

Kenney, Karen. *Immune System.* Minneapolis, MN: Jump!, 2017.

# INTERNET RESOURCES

Infectious Diseases
**https://medlineplus.gov/infectiousdiseases.html**
Hosted by the U.S. Library of Medicine, this site has tons of information about infectious diseases, including different types and how they spread.

Teen Health and Wellness
**http://www.teenhealthandwellness.com/**
A comprehensive site with tons of information about the body and health.

TeensHealth: Immune System.
**http://kidshealth.org/en/teens/immune.html**
A thorough overview of the human immune system, including the different components and how it works to keep us healthy.

---

## Picture Credits:

Page 5: Rost9/Shutterstock.com, 14: Pathdoc/Dreamstime.com, 21: Daniel Dash/Dreamstime.com,
24: rlakov Filimonov/Dreamstime.com, 37: Anut21ng Photo/Dreamstime.com, 58: 7active Studio /Dreamstime.com,
66: Tacio Philip Sansonovski/Dreamstime.com 71: Brian Chase/Dreamstime.com, 74-75: PLRANG ART/Shutterstock.com,
Ralwel/Shutterstock.com, Sebastian Kaulitzki/Shutterstock.com, 76: S K Chavan/Shutterstock.com.
All other images copyrighted by Macaw Books.

# INDEX

## G

gastrointestinal diseases, 19–20
gastrointestinal tract, 18–19, 23
germs, 6–8
   protection against, 8
   types of, 7
giardiasis, 19
glycoproteins. *See* interleukins

## H

halophiles, 9
handwashing, 8
HCl. *See* stomach acid
hemoglobin, 25, 43
hepatitis, 12, 65
histamines, 25
hypothyroidism, 58–59

## I

Ig antibodies. *See* immunoglobulins
immune system, 6–7, 14, 24–30, 40–42
   acquired immunity, 29
   innate immunity, 27
immunodeficiencies, 58–60
immunoglobulins, 22, 30, 46, 52–54
infectious diseases, 64–66
inflammation, 25, 49–51
influenza, 8, 12
interferons, 26
interleukins, 35, 42
Isaacs, Alice, 42

## J

Jenner, Edward, 73

## L

Lagerhan's cells, 36
Landsteiner, Karl, 40
leukocytes, 24–25
   *See also* immune system
lymph, 25, 32
lymph nodes, 32–33
lymphatic fluid, 32

lymphatic system, 31–36
   fluid of, 32
   glands of, 32–33
   organs of, 32
   vessels of, 31
lymphocytes, 26, 30–32
lymphoid cells, 34–36
lymphoid glands, 32–33
lymphoid organs, 32
lysozyme, 22

## M

macrophages, 37–38
major histocompatibility molecules (MHC), 41
malaria, 8, 18–19, 66
marrow, 25–26, 32, 34
mast cells, 38
measles, 30
medication, 8
methanogens, 9
microorganisms. *See specific types*
mucous membranes, 22
mucus, 14
mushrooms, 15
myeloid cells, 37–39
   *See also* phagocytes

## N

natural killer cells
   *See also* lymphocytes
neutrophils, 37, 39
nucleic acid. *See* DNA; RNA

## O

oral thrush, 65

## P

papillomavirus, 21
parasites, 15, 18–19
paratopes, 55
passive immunity, 30
   *See also* immune system; vaccines
Pasteur, Louis, 15
pathogens, 18–19, 27, 30

# INDEX